T0414375

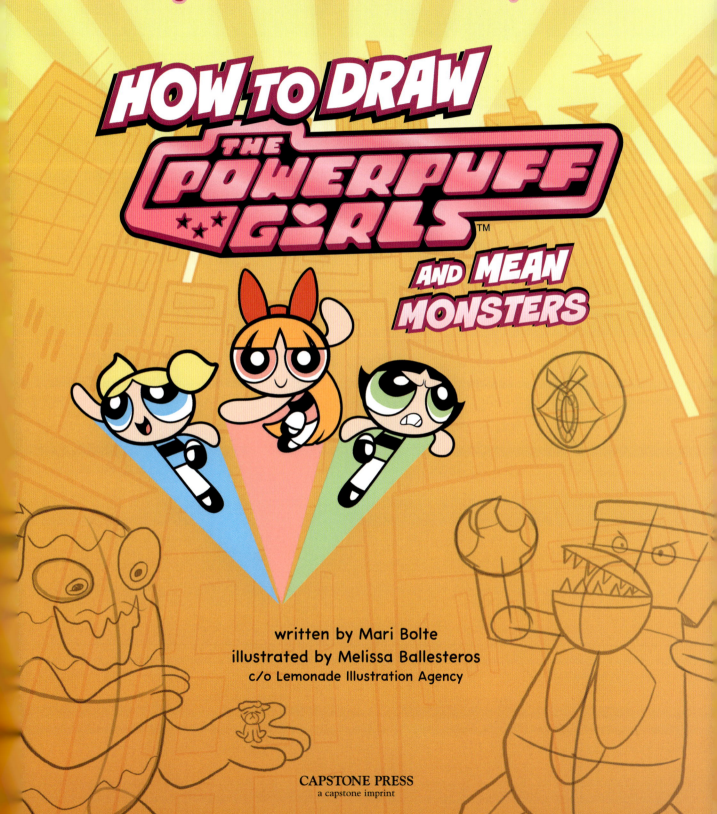

dabble lab

Drawing Adventures with the Powerpuff Girls!

HOW TO DRAW

THE POWERPUFF GIRLS ™

AND MEAN MONSTERS

written by Mari Bolte
illustrated by Melissa Ballesteros
c/o Lemonade Illustration Agency

CAPSTONE PRESS
a capstone imprint

Published by Capstone Press, an imprint of Capstone.
1710 Roe Crest Drive, North Mankato, Minnesota 56003
capstonepub.com

Cataloging-in-Publication Data is available on the Library of Congress website.

ISBN: 9781669075738 (hardcover)
ISBN: 9781669075691 (ebook PDF)

Summary: Go on a drawing adventure with the Powerpuff Girls and their foes!
Young artists of all abilities will have fun as they learn how to draw the monsters of Townsville
alongside Blossom, Bubbles, and Buttercup through easy step-by-step instructions.

Editorial Credits
Editor: Abby Huff; Designer: Hilary Wacholz; Production Specialist: Tori Abraham

Printed and bound in China. 5834

TABLE OF CONTENTS

MEET THE POWERPUFF GIRLS ™

The perfect little girl doesn't exist—

Wait, wait, don't get mad! Let me finish! I was going to say: "The perfect little girl doesn't exist . . . because there are three of them!" Together, Blossom, Bubbles, and Buttercup fight crime and keep the citizens of Townsville safe.

That's no small feat, especially since Townsville sees its fair share of monsters! The creatures come in all shapes and sizes. It's a good thing the Powerpuff Girls aren't afraid to take on the slimiest and spookiest brutes.

Remember, these monsters are only as scary as you make them! Grab your art supplies and begin a brave drawing adventure!

THE CARTOONIST'S TOOLBOX

Anyone can put pen to paper and become a cartoonist. Just follow the steps, practice, and have fun! Here are a few tools and tips on how to bring the Powerpuff Girls and their beastly foes to life.

A **pencil** is one of the best drawing tools around! Keep it sharp. Lightly sketch characters first.

Have an **eraser** handy. You're bound to make mistakes, and that's okay! An eraser can also remove lines from earlier steps and polish up your drawing.

Grab a good fine-tip **black marker**. Trace your drawing when it's just how you like. Allow time for the ink to fully dry so it doesn't smudge.

Add a pop of color! **Colored pencils** and **markers** are great options. Bright colors help your finished drawing shine.

BEWARE: BAD BREATH!

Nothing is worse than morning breath—unless you're the Toilet-Mouthed Monster! He's got a potty mouth, and he's not afraid to use it. That's very, very naughty! Will the Powerpuff Girls put him in time-out, or will he overflow and flood Townsville with foul language?

TIP
Everyone loves picking out a new toothbrush at the dentist. What style would you pick to clean up this monster's dirty mouth? Draw it in!

1

2

3

4

GAME ON, MONSTERS

Check it out! Buttercup is ready to kick some monster heinie. She's the toughest fighter of the sister trio. She's never afraid to jump into a brawl. It's no bluff—it's a Powerpuff! Monsters, beware. Buttercup is on her way!

1

EYE SEE YOU

Look left. Look right. See anything? The Eye Monster can! It's got its eye on everyone and everything. Don't think a quick poke will stop this baddie either. Extra eyeballs on its body are ready to open up. Plus, its laser vision keeps it from getting distracted. Entering a staring contest has never been riskier!

TIP

A V-shaped eyebrow makes this brute look mad. Try turning the eyebrow upside-down. Is the monster less scary?

1

MAGGOT MONSTER MADNESS

Blossom, Bubbles, and Buttercup aren't scared of much. But they really, really, *really* don't like bugs! And a baby bug like this one is even ickier. The Maggot Monster likes to pop up in bad dreams with its evil buddy, the Boogie Man. A good squish should keep this pest away.

TIP

The Maggot Monster wears a big feathered hat. But what if it wants to switch its style? Draw a new hat. Baseball, cowboy, jester . . . any kind will do!

1

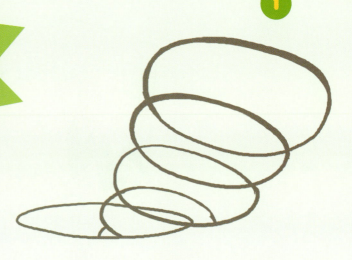

RSVP TO THE BIRTHDAY BOT

Every birthday party needs a giant robot, right? The villain Mojo Jojo sure thinks so. He sent the Birthday Robot to the Powerpuff Girls on their special day. The machine was wrapped up in a box with a bow. Instead of singing to celebrate, the robot went wild! It wrecked the sisters' birthday bash. Watch out for flying cake!

FACT

The Powerpuff Girls have X-ray vision. They tried to peek inside their gifts, but Professor Utonium reminded them: No powers at the present table.

2

3

4

15

CLOUDY WITH A CHANCE OF CHEESE

What's that in the sky? Is it a bird? Is it a plane? No, it's . . . alien broccoli?! The Broccoloids are here to take over the planet! The only way to fight back is by eating your veggies. Luckily, the Powerpuff Girls show the kids of Townsville how to take a bite out of crime. Pass the cheese sauce.

1

TIP
Draw the leader of the Broccoloids! He wears a belt and cape. He holds a staff with a top shaped like broccoli!

2

3

4

MEET THE GANGREEN GANG

Hidden deep inside the Townsville dump is a secret shack. It may be smelly. It may be dirty. But the Gangreen Gang calls it home. Ace is the group's leader. Snake is his sidekick. And Big Billy is the muscle behind the brains. A life of crime suits the gang just fine.

FACT
Big Billy is the only member of the Gangreen Gang who has red hair. His hair hides his eyes.

1

2

3

4

GANGREEN WITH ENVY

The Gangreen Gang isn't complete without Grubber and Lil' Arturo. They may be green and in the gang, but they can still be classy. Grubber doesn't only scare people for fun. He also plays the violin and speaks with a British accent! Lil' Arturo drinks coffee . . . and then gains super speed! Try keeping up with him after an espresso.

TIP

Each Gangreen Gang boy has a different hand style. Pay attention to the shapes. Those details give a character more personality.

1

BLOWUP BALLOON

Something is living in the lake. It won't nibble toes or tip over boats. But it will go on a mad rampage through Townsville! Using its huge mouth to suck in air, the Giant Fish Balloon can blow itself up to the size of a dinosaur. But like a balloon, it can be deflated just as easily. *POP!*

FACT
This big fish is covered in spikes. When the monster is full of air, its spikes shoot off in all directions.

23

HERE, KITTY, KITTY

Don't get between the Slime Monster and his kitty cat! The monster nearly flattened Townsville when he realized his fuzzy, fluffy *pwecious* was missing. Talk about a temper tantrum! Make sure that this never happens again. Pencil in the *purr*-fect friend every time you sketch the mound of muck.

1

TIP
The Slime Monster's goo is always on the move. Use wavy lines to show the dripping layers that flow down his body.

THE MONSTER MASH

The Powerpuff Girls face off against many beastly baddies. Each has its own strengths and weaknesses. Some are solid and spiky. Others are squishy and slimy. So be on guard, Blossom! Getting stuck in sludge while saving the day would be really embarrassing.

FACT

The Powerpuff Girls are girls of action! Whether it's a signature kick or fierce uppercut, they've got a finishing move ready to go.

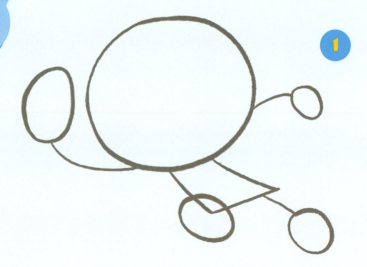

1

ORANGE YOU GLAD FOR ORANGES?

The Amoeba Boys want to be the masterminds behind the biggest crimes ever. Unfortunately, their brains are the size of bacteria. Bossman, Slim, and Junior's most successful heist? When they stole every orange in Townsville. People then got scurvy, like pirates of old! (Not that the Amoeba Boys planned for that to happen.) Someone call the Pow-*Arrrrrr*-puff Girls before we all have to walk the plank right to the doctor's office.

TIP

The Amoeba Boys don't have arms, legs, or hair. But each has a unique body shape. And their hats make it easy to tell them apart!

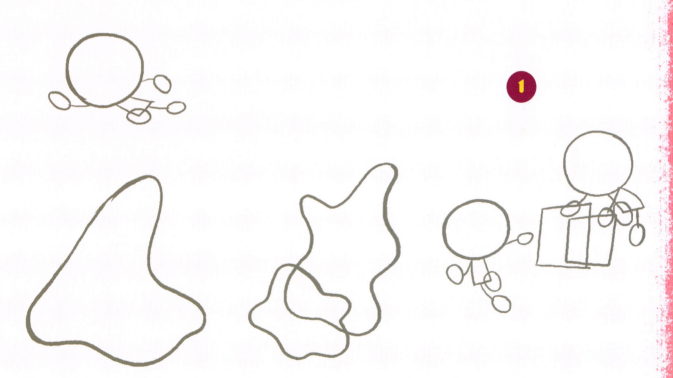

FACT
Townsville is home to many clever crooks . . . and also the Amoeba Boys. They may not be smart, but they're always up for trying a new crime!

READ MORE

Kistler, Mark. *Half Hour of Pencil Power: Fast and Fun Drawing Lessons for the Whole Family!* New York: Hachette Go, 2022.

Korté, Steve. *Draw Scooby-Doo!: Monsters, Robots, Aliens, and More.* North Mankato, MN: Capstone Press, 2022.

Nguyen, Angela. *How to Draw Cute Beasts.* New York: Sterling Children's Books, 2020.

ABOUT THE AUTHOR

Mari Bolte is an author and editor of children's books. Whether it's a book on video games, animals, history, science, monsters, or crafts, she's always up for learning new things. (And hoping readers learn something too!) Mari lives in Minnesota with her family and far too many pets.

ABOUT THE ILLUSTRATOR

Melissa Ballesteros is an illustrator from Guadalajara, Mexico. She is best known for her work in the animation industry. Her background in film studios is shown through her use of vibrant color palettes and energetic characters, a style that also perfectly lends itself to the world of children's book publishing.